Self-Portrait
with a
Million Dollars

Also by Patricia Clark

Poetry Books

The Canopy

Sunday Rising

She Walks into the Sea

My Father on a Bicycle

North of Wondering

Chapbooks

Deadlifts

Wreath for the Red Admiral

Given the Trees

Self-Portrait
with a
Million Dollars

Patricia Clark

Terrapin Books

Terrapin Books
4 Midvale Avenue
West Caldwell, NJ 07006

www.terrapinbooks.com

ISBN: 978-1-947896-27-7
LCCN: 2020936887

First Edition

Redux Series

Cover Art, *Darn*, oil on panel, 50 x 42 inches, 2014
© Mary McDonnell
www.marymcdonnellart.com

for my sister Jean Stewart,
for her early and steady encouragement

and for Stan Krohmer, always

Contents

I only went out for a walk and finally concluded
to stay out till sundown, for going out,
I found, was really going in.
—John Muir

It is like what we imagine knowledge to be:
dark, salt, clear, moving, utterly free.
—Elizabeth Bishop

Coaster

If a gift could mark a time, if a square
of some ceramic substance backed with cork
could be the emblem of a turn, then this

nails it—four inches by four, a creamy tan
and stamped on its face the Puget Sound
map and all the cities of my heart.

Sailing chart, shown with depths, as though
useful for navigation—land painted orange,
water shown in white with inlets in blue.

If it doesn't go far enough north, or most
especially west to Port Angeles, La Push,
still it makes explicit what is lost, sore.

Sibling chart, too, of who lives where—
Olympia, Lacey, Tacoma—everyone else
to the north and two exiles, Chris and me.

To rest a coffee cup upon, to steady a hand.
Flying in this time, seeing the Rockies, brown,
and then the Cascade Mountains—angular, sharp,

with valleys filled up with tumbled fog, thick,
as though it were soup. Ladle this, I tried
to say, each time overcome by something large

the mountains seemed to pull out of me, knowing
it was there, fearing my eyes would fill right
then in the aisle seat of row thirty-two.

Escarpment, arête—it's where you must stand
to look out and down, the most dangerous foothold of all—
the past in front of you like a map, no-map, the slope

precipitous, basalt, pumice lapilli, glass.

I

Feasting, Then

High in the canopy,
feasting, then

falling. A controlled
drop in flight

to a lower branch.
I watched

without understanding,
with awe.

I've been shut in
those houses
too or blind
at work,
not noticing.

All the inattention
when a miracle
takes place nearby

and could save us.
Do I really mean
save? You must

believe me—the feasting
on some tree fruit
high up—and the

bird?—I think
either a flycatcher
or a waxwing.

Such moves, so much
cascading, in
confidence, such lifting
of the beak to sing.

Yes, I mean save.

After the Suicides

We had to go on without you, rise to work,
open the checkbook and balance the funds,

there was laundry to be bundled to the basement,
shoved in the washer, someone forgetting just how

terribly the spin cycle ends, how it leaves jeans sopping,
though they eventually dried out to be hauled

upstairs, and the living room collected dust
on surfaces, dog hair stuck to the rug, clutter of books,

and the kitchen, hearth of it all, hub of life, there
spinach was old, florets of broccoli gone yellow,

icemaker welded the ice into cubes-in-a-field,
potatoes had eyes, fish past its prime,

and yet out of what was edible, someone wrought
a meal into shape, a simple pasta sauce,

an invented bit with mushrooms, onion, cream
poured over tricolor fettucine or angel hair,

that made us laugh, angels indeed, yes
there was red wine from Tuscany, one of us

set the table, smoothed the cloth, removed
the crumbs and we sat together, a candle's light

flickering but holding, the draft didn't wink
it out, around our talk most ordinary, blessed

by a tone of kindness we each adopted
without discussion, lots of please and thanks

as we handed food around, basket of steaming bread
for buttering, and we knocked glasses, looking

each other right in the eye, lovers, opponents, friends
too, agreeing in courage, unvoiced, for another day.

Big White Streak

There, smeared across blue sky, moving east,
widening to dissipate. The thickest part
a cotton roll of banked cloud. Then it starts
attenuating, thinning to a mere haze.
Oh, stay, you hear yourself cry out.
Linger with me against the wide empty
gulf of blue, staring pitilessly back at me.

Provenance

What do you think my necklace
is made of, she asked.

Something from the sea, someone guessed.
Abalone, sea shell.

Or perhaps used button turned
on a lathe.

No, the teeth of camels. That was
her answer. And we talked about
the personalities of camels and llamas
there in the living room.

If you comb a llama's fur, stroking,
it will hum. And it might

puff out air, softly, like a young
child blowing out a candle.

They spit, though, someone said.
And I remembered the female llama
of a friend that ate the male llama's
genitals.

There was a history to it.
Of aggression and nipping.

And we lifted forks, then, and ate
mixed berry pie. Delicious,
someone said.

A little sour, then sweet.

Love Song for Physics and the Nude

after Mathias Alten's Nude with Amaryllis

When news broke that the fabric of space/time
rippled, making an audible chirp, you were still
fresh and nude, your brunette hair tinged with blue,

and the scallop of a curtain revealed cobalt blue
sky, but that was not the story. A white rumpled bed
of pillows, sheets, a royal blue blanket lay arranged

as your throne. The trumpet blooms—there were three—
of the amaryllis opened just a millimeter more,
dropping a scattering of golden pollen grains

onto the soil of the pot. But the real acclaim
and news was how as a woman you rose there, frank,
blushing, bold in your pose, without a name

yet known by us all as a goddess of morning light,
a glowing pillar, small breasts eager to be touched,
believing, as we do, that this moment will stay,

lasting in paint, as the house on Fulton Street stands,
the way black holes, vanished a billion years, left an
effect, and you do as well, your gaze now meeting ours.

Should

Someone should pay in large green bills
with a gold credit card with a sky high
limit, someone should pay for how
this year the season of winter brought
us down, lasted way longer than normal,
left our driveways snow covered, our hands
with cracked skin near the ends of fingers,
someone should pay with their pain
(can we make them pay?) for how many times
we said the name of the ones in power
we despise, a nickel a name, a dime
a time, and we'd be rich, we'd move
out of this country, start over in Split
near the Baltic Sea or in Zagreb, not
that far away, or choose a more popular place
like Ireland or Canada. Let's ratchet it up:
someone should have to pay for just how
we've been upset, tipped on our sides,
made unable to sleep with worry over bombs,
human rights, racism, deportation, and very large
insults to our intelligence along with parks
being sold, trees cut down, pollution allowed
to go on unchecked. People in Flint,
in Michigan, near where we live, they want
clean water, an end to pipes lined with lead.
What, you say, a lot of the world lives just
this way? Maybe at last it's coming through
clearly—it's not just us, others treated worse.
We had to listen to the dreadful names,
see their faces, but we had a warm house

to go back to at night, food in the fridge,
and eventually we fell asleep, a dog
at the bedside, while you, and I mean you
the majority had no bed in which to sleep.

Coveting the River Birch

Because the bark peels off,
it flays itself and allows
the inner surfaces to be
seen and known—

A papery bark that is white
on the outside.
Peeled back, the inner
surface has a blush

or peach color—an
admission of how
private this side is.
Three birches in one

group, two in the other.
To stand together
is to shield oneself a bit
from scrutiny.

I could be that brave
peel back and show.
After years on guard
finally open to bracing touch.

In Praise of the Dickcissel

O small meadowlark,
o bunting,

bird with gold on your
crown and breast,

a black vee, some chestnut
on your wings, you love

meadows and savannas,
red-tipped grass, you

perch there, swaying, in
sunny grassland

near the wastewater
treatment plant,

the shit, the clogged
plastic from pipes, drains,

toilets, and the raw
stink that's on the wind.

The smell catches in our
hair, clothes, fills

the car that is our
blind to approach you.

O bird, you own these
nearby fields and dusty

road where we saw,
too, an upland sandpiper.

You endure it, and we'll do
the same, imperfect

stinking world, grassland
and the marginal place

where beauty dwells.
The strawberry moon has come

and gone, at home our
garden with basil, fennel,

parsley, chives grows leggy,
not yet the harvest, not

yet time for birds to
fly away. O stay, dickcissel,

singing where you
sway, till your throat burns.

After you've flown,
what will we do,

who or what will
console us?

Canine Elegy

All over town, dogs are lying down
for the last time—how many bright balls
lost in grass, Frisbees sent spinning on air?

What shall be done with crate and leash,
collar, basket of toys, blanket for sitting in the car?
All over town, dogs are lying down.

We mark her life as she left, in turn,
marks on things she chewed—Christmas tree string
of lights, chair legs—and on us, too.

She never dug holes in the yard, refused to run
after the woodchuck I told her to chase, or kill.
She bolted once or twice after deer.

All over town, dogs are lying down
for the final time—who do we grieve for,
them, or ourselves? We scrub their bowls,

the rug, hang up the leash. Will there be
a next dog? Mostly, she did anything I asked—
jumped a hurdle, or leapt onto a fallen log.

If ever I hurt her, it was an accident—foot I stepped on
in the dark, hair clipped too close. Dogs are lying down
to rest, forever, all over town: Molly, Raef, and Scout—

giving up their last breaths, leaving us to applaud
how avid for life they were even as eyes
clouded, hips gave way on stairs. Images stay:

dog pushing her muzzle into snow, licking the face
of a veteran hunched in a wheelchair at the park, or
sitting to let a child touch her velvet ear.

Fur lies in corners of the house, sticky like
burs on clothes. Dogs are lying down in places all
over town, and us with them, at the last.

Ragged

Warm wooden leg of a table,
       August sun, and the red admiral

staying there, flexing its wings,
       yellow pear tomatoes turning gold,

hour by hour, and the woods, still
       green, but somehow more somber

each day, though I try staying just
       here in this moment, breathing,

watching, living—what part of us wants
       to measure or compare? This year

against last, this year's tomato yield
       over last? I lean back in the red chair

soaking up heat, I touch the dog's
       black silky ear—we are specks

in this speck of time—tonight, the Perseids—
       we whirl together just for now,

this dance, this stardust, light on a wing.

Controlled Burn

It came in the mail, an official-
looking letter with the seal
of our government, or at least

the county agency in charge
of setting fires, putting them out.
It described a strip of land

across the highway from us,
they defined what a swale was,
saying this is it—and they told

what they hoped to burn out,
though now my memory grows
uncertain—mustard garlic, for one,

purple loosestrife, perhaps, and a plant
called knuckleweed, maybe, or was it
knucklehead? They wanted us to know,

to stay clear of the area on a certain
date, or to object in writing if we had
concerns. Their promises grew

large: the watershed would be enlarged,
color and flavor of the water improved,
and I'm sure they said we would all

sleep better at night, though that seems
a stretch. It came about just as they
said—the date came and passed, we saw

a little smoke, nothing more. One day
we drove over just to see—and the strip
once green was now burnt black, a sign

told the tale. Our water never changed
and our dreams were as fractured
as before. No one I knew remembered a thing.

Near the Tea House at Meijer Japanese Garden

Beyond the leaf, the pea gravel path,
what stays with me

is moving water, the deer-startling
fountain with its bamboo trough,

a slender sloping throat,
clatter of bucket into water,

and the tea house with its spare
rooms, windows without glass.

If I could walk here on a full moon
night, I would invite

my spirit double to join me,
she who scuttles away

like a hermit crab, whose wrist
I'd like to hold, pulse

I'd like to feel. There's a tender
part of her I need,

now tracing a pale blue vein
under skin like a leaf's midrib.

II

Threnody

You never had a chance
                              to speak, pressed under and down
            by weight of water.

Bend close to me now—and listen.

Sometimes you toiled at work—oiler, deckhand,
                              captain, mate—pulled down in a fight
            to save your ship on blizzard seas. Ore carriers plowing thick
waves
            on the Great Lakes, those inland waters where a fetch builds up
                              intensity crossing three hundred miles
of open water, ships racing to get in a last
voyage: ice gripping the gunnels, the rudder and prow.

Or you were driving home, highway a lit ribbon
                              through cornfields, past dunes, jostling
            in the car with your friends. Who suggested
            a quick swim in Lake Michigan?
Did you three feel a thrill as you splashed into cold water?

Can anyone answer why you didn't know
                              what a red flag flying
            above the beach meant, and how to escape?
                              Girl, the newspaper carried your photo
days until they found your body.

Or you kicked your way in, racing to save someone,
                              desperate to reach your own child
            or a sister, brother, in water so shallow
            you could see white sand at the bottom.

Did it comfort you at all,
unable to loosen small fingers from your arms
or neck, that you'd go down together?

Music along the shore, wind that moans
                              passing lighthouse, jetty, snow fence,
        shoreward pines. And pebbles rolling
in the surf, colliding, roaring, hitting.

I wonder if you see now that words are not
                              enough to bring you back
from the other side—.

Sand mixes with the lake becoming
                              clay, becoming ash.

Along the high-water mark, discarded items
        of the lost—bracelet, shoe,
        particle of a life, a song, word, note.

If we ask, do not haunt us, do not
                              come again.

                    We have heard you, voices
from the deep—now we let you go.

Ravine Idyll

The sun-dappled ravine floor has a crunch to it.
Last year's leaves break apart and down.
There is this day, cooler, with more of summer to come.

The sun-dappled ravine floor still flows green.
Last week I saw a doe and fawn lie down.
Not yet the turn, not yet a painted leaf.

The ravine floor has a supple give, good moist earth.
Paths cross it where fox and white tails walk.
Change in the air, this moment cannot last.

The charge: note what is here, what departs,
and do not fall to mourning, for this, or
us. In the meadow, goldenrod, fragrant when crushed.

Les Rochers de Belle-Ile

after the painting by Claude Monet

No beach here—just the sea
swirling in blue

deep blue and green

Both the sea and the rocks
show age

It's a tired scene of their
coming together

each hour and day

The water's force, erosion
of all the softest parts

leaving only solid rock

This you could be
crushed upon—the hardest

knowledge of all—

What is impervious to you, quite
solidly indifferent

No escaping how the sea

throws you repeatedly on the rocks
of all you're stupid about—

self-ignorance, deception, lies—

Instead someone calls this a scene,
a landscape, seascape—

yes, but first: crags of the mind, and soul.

Diptych with Window View & Hiroshige Print

No tree vaulting high that I could see
possessed a perfectly straight trunk.

> *A geisha follows a trail of paper lanterns.*

Yellow leaves had been blown off,
leaving black branches.

> *Stars in water a match for the sky.*
> *A windless night, and all clear.*

Something was coming, the wind a portent.

> *A red petticoat peaked out from under her coat.*

Deer hid and wild turkeys latched onto a roost.

> *Near the hill's foot, a shrine and brightly lit restaurants.*

Solitary means to turn in
on yourself, a whelk, and no escape.

> *A cropped lantern, cropped cherry tree, and still she walks*
> *in dignity, with purpose.*

The gusts came from the east,
blowing saplings in half.

> *Behind her, the Sumida River, a sky of stars,*
> *stars in the river, and beyond, a black hill.*

My Last Brother's Last Son

drives off to college, leaving behind
Douglas firs, rocky beaches of Puget
Sound for Half Moon Bay, Bodega
Bay, and California sun. Will he return?

My brother's last son goes off,
we're all empty nesters now
whether we had kids or not,
same footing, same grief,

rooms where we live gathering
dust, mattresses and pillows holding
the shapes of who's gone, a few
shoes left in closets, books, an old

dog pining in the fenced yard.
When my last brother's last son
goes off, driving away, we find ourselves
grieving too, another childhood gone,

a wife or husband to look at
over coffee, wondering where did we
leave off, when is the last time
we sat together, talking, intimate?

My brother's two sons go away
in different directions, one goes east,
the other goes south down the coast,
they're both playing music loud,

it's all about joy, mostly theirs, some ours,
but it drowns out conveniently the worry,
grief too, no more going back,
Commencement Bay, only a sure track

moving ahead. When Michael's last
son goes away, I remember the year
he was born, not his son but him,
our mother forty-two and birthing a kid

started from an old egg—she without fear.
No genetic testing for her. Michael arriving
in a squall, perfect and whole, last boy, ten
fingers and toes, carrot-red hair.

When my last brother's last son goes away
there's quiet in bedroom, kitchen, halls, the yard,
our hearts, space to let the unknown in,
to grasp what comes next—the dog lies
        down at the gate.

My Beautiful Family

I stood watching a whole flock of dark birds
winging this way—

squawking as they rowed,
steering to avoid me.

Beyond lies Lamberton Creek, August slow
and flat. Not a ripple or rill.

And what is this air fragrant
with berries, ripened, fallen,
and the fat ears of corn in fields,
not to mention the tomato
           hanging low, a gash chewed out?

That she passed away, no one
thinking to tell us—
           try to pretend, now,

this isn't an insult,

that our time together
wasn't an illusion, a television show
of a family at Thanksgiving—
           the turkey carved from cardboard,
mashed potatoes made from dryer lint.

Mystery of a singer near, in the white oak,
identity unknown,
                   clear line of elegy,
each note a dark pearl.

Oyster Shell (toward an *Ars Poetica*)

One side a cup, glissando
of silky white.

The other gnarled, pocked
as though to keep

you out. Ruffled
edge, layered like sediment

in a canyon, lit up,
here dentistry of gray.

What lay here in this
bowl of white-purple-gold

mother-of-pearl is
gone with no trace.

I can see its plump
gray-black body and let

my tongue explore the faint
salt tang, smell of kelp

waving in the sea
as though to lure

me deeper. O, I would
taste again,

be drawn down,
in, with ocean

roaring forte
in flooded ears.

Sibelius While an Oak Topples

I turn it up loud,
louder, to mask

the chain saw's
cough and steady

whine, the noise
of the workmen

hollering, the dull
thuds when one

throws down a chunk
of trunk or limb.

What do we do,
living in this

world—my neighbor
who fears the oak

will fall, crush
his boy where he lies

sleeping. I didn't
make the world

of chain-link fence,
bark collar, leash,

bite of the chainsaw,
the woman on the news

who crept out on ice
to rescue her dog,

then fell through,
scrabbling for a way

out. I, too, wanted silence—
look at me using a melodic

impromptu to hide
horror, kick and bite

of the saw, the dog's
jerk to get away

from the jolt
of what they call

"the correction," and yes,
I think she called

for help, woman who
had laughed at work

with kids on the blacktop
playground (they talked

to one boy on the news).
I am not as immune

from pain as I try
to pretend, my chest

felt sore and I touched
Josie's fur, looking in her

eyes, seeing another
creature trying to breathe,

to play with a ball,
or lie in peace on the rug

when the sun streaks in,
promising to last.

The workmen will grind
the stump when they

finish, and the boy sleeps
on. The woman's dog

scrambled off the ice,
safely, and ran home,

that's how her family
knew to go looking. They sail

another chunk down using
a pulley, thud, ground trembles,

goes still. They found
her body there, shards

broken around the hole.
The children said she

played with them every
day at recess. Even now

Josie's learning not
to bark, just one soft

one to sound an alarm,
then she stops.

Those at the Edge of Water

The rake pulled across white gravel has left
its marks, furrows of thought in parallel lines
that flow around rocks like a river's

eddies—one rock could be a bridge,
another a boat. Today could be the end—
the last warm day of the year. Is it

enough to note how golden leaves fall,
in a week they will be gone, or is there
more to say? Those who built gardens

in fifteenth-century Japan were a class
of pariahs, non-humans, called *kawaramono*,
translated as *those at the edge of the water*.

How many washed away by yearly floods,
how many bending their backs, lifting hands
to dig communal graves along the water's edge?

Outcasts without names, they learned bold
ways of placing stones or planting a tree.
Each leaf that falls I name one of them

gone, there goes another on the breeze, a waft,
a fall. By week's end, hardwoods, oaks
will be bare. The last warm day, a rake

drawn through gravel is making lines, curves.

Mallards at Rest

The woods regal in copper, russet,
      gold, and the air seemingly spun gold

though it is November. Over planks
      of the bridge, we cross the lagoon where

down below, along water's edge, mallards
      have tucked wings, feathers and heads. Only

green on their crowns shows. I know any
      moment they could startle up into

ducks—for now they linger as feathers
      over warm bodies asleep in a

world easily able to harm them.
      Like sleeping children or any group

of innocents, let them rest for now—
      the dispossessed, lost, astray, wayward

travelers who, if they can find peace
      for a nap, in shade, let them be.

After Failure

When it happens, or not, when you soar or fall,
when you step out past the lilac, the red oak,
       you see it, or you don't.

When the sky goes from aubergine to black,
when you stare west-south-west and it comes,
       the space station glowing steady as your heartbeat.

Here is the table set with linens, silver, glass,
here is the blush of wine, rosé from France,
       a plate of olives and the salt.

Did you think it would be easy, that the rub
       of pumice would remove the callus,
       that you could spit on your palms,
       set to work, break the impasse?

When the trap is set, you can't turn back,
       though already any zeal you had
       for cornering the bear is gone—

When you find, instead, a hole in your heart,
       sympathy for the wren, not to mention
       the boy in your class, congenital, fatal.

When you raise your eyes, the sky a blotch,
       clouds broken as everything else,
when the den appears empty, the ursine
       creature vanished in a whiff of scent.

When you could curl into a ball but don't,
when you see the earth like a single cell
        and places near water or not,

Oman to Rome, Seattle to Boston harbors,
East Coast and then way east to Liverpool and more,
        when you see landscapes there, tread

the dock, smell kelp and salt from ocean waves, remember
        people, the good bread and solid matter of work,

potatoes to be peeled, wine poured, mess of a kitchen tidied up,
        you refuse defeat, eyes growing steely, back straightening,
        and like a spider spinning her web, mind crafting a plan.

III

When the Hawk Refuses to Fly

When the wind ratcheted up, tuning its howl,
I left my small hut under the white pine,

preferring the house and its heat, its full
kitchen and stock of candles, matches, books.

I also left a couple of pecker-fretted trees,
sure to fall, and the fifty-foot red oak,

sure to last. If I eat two clementines a day,
will they ward off what could be coming?

Dark enough I can't name it—very sly
and pernicious, maybe something in DNA,

blood, marrow of the bone. The hawk, sharp-
shinned, refuses to fly in this weather, staying

on its nest, swaying there, and the lost
seeds of perennials go scattering off

to dry places where they'll bloom next year.
Surprised at volunteers, we forget the wind.

The house rides low to the ground, hugging
it for stability, a smooth sail through the night.

Above the racket of tree limbs clattering, bone
bucket, an oak's trunk groans like a man down.

At Random, I Open the Book on Waking, Dreaming, Being to the Chapter on Dying

It's a day ahead on my calendar
shielded in mystery,

                how odd, I think,

and how wondrous.

If I could learn not to fear it,
if I could embrace it.

                I look out on this day—

gray shuttering down the green, filled
with birdsong, mostly cardinals and a lone wren—
and a sudden downpour

                of heavy drops.

That brought out the robins—to sip
up the rain from the driveway.

                In this way,

everything is useful. When I go,
some extra air will be around
to be breathed

                by somebody else.

Maybe an orca, or a child.
Maybe a grizzled dog.

I Am Going to Start Living Like a Zen Priest

Slipping into my cork-soled sandals,
I enter the garden through the tall gate.

If I step and bend with the right
posture, I believe the scarlet tanager

will reveal itself to me again, having no
ambition beyond letting its crimson

profile and dark wings fill my eyes.
Two tasks present themselves to me—

wrestle some plants, first, into the twin
window boxes at my hut, ones tall

and spiky, and flowing ones, purple as rich
robes of an emperor. My other,

harder, task is to bring a cascading flow
of coolness into the range of my ear.

My failing is getting ahead of myself
at times—I have the tall fat-bellied pot

in muted gray, and I've balanced the bamboo
fountain in it, testing the electric pump.

The base must be built—a masonite square,
treated pine lengths for the sides, and tumbled

black polished river stones. These will be set
on edge, lined up in rows in clean sand.

My brain rests like water, calm, clear—
I gather trowel, watering can, and go.

Grand Marais Estuary, in Fog

after the painting by Stanley Krohmer

Color of ice, or heaps of snow, gray-blue, slate.
Texture enough to point out land, two spots,

but catalog the rest as sky, wave, or in-between
where all reside, even us. How far

we've come from home to stay at a hilltop
cabin riven with mice, brush burs

from the dog's coat, find a place in town
to eat whitefish and hear the tales

while the proprietor pours pinot noir
noting our clothing, hair, and diction

as non-U.P. but still acceptable to him.
We made the pilgrimage when Jim was still

alive, regaled him with one or two repeated
stories—one about *Ulysses*, another a sledge

struck at a deer. Or was it a bear, in town?
The place laps on without him now, the bay,

the bars, and in our town a stand of staghorn
sumac turning red again where we took

photos of him and us—the giant a monument
before collapse, sprawled across his studio floor.

After the Darkest Year

Out of verdant and lush,
oak leaf, Virginia creeper vine,
blackberry wild as today's wind,
sumac, invasive honeysuckle,
each different leaf a knuckle, earlobe, or palm
of the hand,

in thirty days no less, from dormant
to swaying, leaves shivering and trembling,
one side grayer, one side slick,
shiny on top,

and what gets through of sunlight
dappled and shade-crazed,
sunburst down to a single blade
standing tall on ravine-floor,
leaf-pile, leaf mold, crackle
of still dried stalk and spent
blossom trundled from the yard,

an ancient process, green
to done, down, trampled on, spent,
left here to vegetate, pack deep
under snow, decompose,
and then all starts again,

warbler time just after dormancy breaks,
bud swell and pencil point unfurling
of green, each blossom and ear leaf
sparking in its time—trillium, may-
apple, redbud, lilac, more—

and the welcome scents
lively on the air, fresh and new
as any flower, note of honey,
jasmine, vanilla, lemon, bark,

till all is filled, unfurled, spread wide
and out—umbrella canopy, wand of
Solomon's seal with berries white,
dangling, ripe—and whose mouth
will surround, pull them off to eat?

So sudden you could blink, miss it, lose
sight of dame's rocket imagining it
phlox when it's not, lavender, white,
and pink covering a slope, a hill,
an elevated bank by the creek
or by the busy road usually all dun
and trash, dirt, dust, but now
a gorgeous swell, in bloom, so brief.

Garden at St. Remy: An Assay

Our guide, Anna-Luce, says she can't
say Van Gogh like "Van, go!"

                Her guttural words
blow away on the mistral wind.

She cracks a joke about escapes
from prison by helicopter,
                    pointing at overhead wires.

We pass fields of golden rapeseed,
poplar and cypress planted to block the wind.

Outside the buildings at St. Remy,
lilacs bloom in purple and white,
                  wisteria hang thick as grapes,

the lavender is not yet blooming,
nor the poppies, in vivid orange.

             Is this a bench where
       Vincent sat to think? Did he roam
          here, seeking solace?

Anna-Luce says he was haunted
from childhood by another Vincent, dead
brother of the same name.

His history, ours, there are
ghosts everywhere—

The mistral lifts dust
in spirals, twisted, rising,

like a man's shape walking.

Psychology of Travel

By season's end, the wasp is dead,
windowboxes have rotted out, chartreuse

leaves of potato vine lie chewed by deer.
Did you think booking a trip to Paris

would disguise the malaise? If you light
a candle, try to startle your heart awake

by kissing a coffin, you can do it,
whispering the word *étoile*, trying to hug

neighbor or friend just to feel warmth.
See your doppelganger? Can you spar

with her? She'll try to tie you in knots—
slip out of her grasp, fix a stare on her.

Oh honey, you whisper to her, I love the way
you maintain the façade: not twins

or even likenesses. Don't interfere while I
line brows or lips, *maquillaje* how I greet

the day. My heart's now solid bronze.
I change my destination to Bangladesh

where the water's rising as I write, mauve
sky at dusk, bay bubbling with eels.

The Trees Did Nothing

A teenage boy, drunk, on pills, careened
off the road, smashed headfirst into a tree.

Deputies driving behind him managed
to drag him out of the burning car.
If you thought pastoral meant

shepherds wandering out to comfort
the injured or that a red maple

tried sending moisture to douse flames,
well, no. If you thought snowbanks

acted as buffer, blanket, balm,
wrong again. A broken right leg
caused him to scream—better

than going up in flames. Both maple
and boy will show scars—

both will die, years hence, with them.
Pastoral has the emphasis on the first
syllable—it's long ago, gone,

and the keening moan you hear,
well, it's the leftover icy wind.

Barred Owl

Before the dark-eyed owl came, flying
toward me, I was going to quit for the day.

It flew, a bird of many feathers, I stayed,

and before the dog roused, with its bark and bite,
I sank down feelers into sandy soil,

I planted footings, one on every corner,

enough to be level, balanced, and still
portable. I could be moved, I could be

nomad, and for the first time in four or

five years, I sensed a breathing on my own,
a careless way of throwing down sweater, scarf,

bracelet or book, this moment for swooping deep

into silence, carried on a magical chair—
to a space rarely visited, newly found,

where thought is a lush country, fragrant, wide.

Kubota Garden

I wanted to see the tea house
a bridge arching over water

I wanted to study Japanese maples
their fine-toothed fiery leaves

I wanted to bow my head to chance,
to a lantern, to stones placed in a wall

The paths led us down and down
far off we heard workmen building a road
overhead a jet scrawled a contrail note of farewell

If I wanted to kneel at the pond, it was to know
how like my mother I've become

I wanted to admire hydrangeas, exclaim
at a lace-cap two-color one—both blush pink

and purple, on one stem—taking a photo to share—
I wanted to touch the clapper in the bronze bell

at the gate, where two panels slide together,
each side making one half of the sun—

letting it sound and then be still

IV

Thank a Gardener, a Perennial, a Bee

A sedum variety
called Live Forever. Its knack:
it regenerates from the
least bit left—fragment of stem,
leaf, pistil, flower. The book
calls it *coarse* which seems an insult
until you note it applies
to leaves. And hear details of
flowers—star-like at the end
of succulent stalks. Isn't
that where the best of most things
is found? It flourishes in
disturbed areas, roadsides,
open woods from Newfoundland
to Ontario, if you
go east to west. Children play
with leaf layers forming small
balloon purses. Maryland
to the south, north to Wisconsin.
Four-petalled flowers form what
are called *terminal clusters*.
I knew they had hidden dark
notes!—in truth, the flowers die.
Still, they were star-like, stardust,
as we were, while they lasted.

When I Stepped Out

a female Baltimore oriole blew past
going the other way, toward suet and house,

rowing at quite a clip, and my thoughts streamed
the other way, toward freedom, water, green.

What do we know of others we live among?
When the barred owl stared back from a branch

through coal-dark eyes, I wondered what it thought—
was it a simple calculation of prey, not prey?

Or was I sized up as definitely other, one of the box-
dwellers who turn on the lights at dusk?

Not to mention the garter snake our dog faced
off with, out back at the woodpile, or the turtle

at the Grand River burying her eggs in sand.
Who are we all, and more urgently, why?

My niece mentioned she took medication—first
I'd heard, and hundreds of unshared facts

about ourselves lined up numerous as books
on my shelves or spices arranged on racks.

Migratory, the orioles arrive each spring
announced by tendrils of song that wake us

in our beds. A box-dweller, I'll take the name—
with a predilection to roost among oaks, and sing.

For the Atlas Moth

Your life of only three days
began far from jungles
of Southeast Asia,

and I mourn the loss
of greenery, your waking up
on display in a plexiglass

hatching booth in the northern
hemisphere, Grand Rapids,
Michigan, to be exact.

Moth, I admire the chestnut
brown-white-and-black
swirls and spots of your

beautiful wings, large as
palm leaves, your thick
unsegmented body, antennae,

noting how like a snake's
head—one about to strike—
the marks have been

made, a painting drawn
to confuse predator birds.
Where you attached yourself—

glass sterile between us—
I raised my hand—
each wing larger than that.

In flight a wingspan
greater than one foot—
a humbling shadow cast.

When the chirpy volunteer
said, "Note that it has no
mouth," my sorrow began

deepening—your time spent
being born, drying those
gorgeous wings, the hurry

to find a mate—that fumbling
in dark haste, lying
together and then dying.

Will you find a mate
here among tropical ferns,
banana plants, colorful

orchids of purple,
gold, and white?
How much does your DNA

long for salt sea air
of Asia? My questions
trail beyond your life.
I offer them as elegy.

Doughnut Ghazal

How easily our happiness bloomed—*doughnuts*
the word Father said. "She's gone. Let's make doughnuts."

She was off giving birth, May '65, to red-headed Michael.
Father assembled ingredients for deep frying doughnuts.

As the army trained him, he cleaned the kitchen first.
He had the cookbook open: beignets, crullers, doughnuts.

Two eggs, sugar in a sparkling mound, one cup
of milk. He had a secret touch for making doughnuts.

How little we knew of supper night after night, meal
plan, vitamins, casserole. Our taste was for doughnuts.

Another time it was rock salt and ice, making peach ice cream.
Happy to turn the crank. Fun, like deep frying doughnuts.

O! when she returned, it was asparagus, lima beans, peas.
Patricia wanted another kid—let Father make doughnuts.

Every Spider I Save Could Be the Instrument

Outside the glass, there's
a red spider climbing
the chain of its web
up and down
plus sometimes

swinging sideways
like a tiny Tarzan
action figure
except it is not
Tarzan but a red

spider about the size
of a peppercorn
before you put it
in the red pepper grinder,
turning the handle

to make the black
bits of it fall onto
your food adding
to its zest, giving
it a little bite

Earlier another spider,
this time, black,
startled me as it
crawled the kitchen
sink—I surprised

myself by saving
its life, putting my
favorite gray and black
cup over it, using
the lawyer's bill

in a stiff envelope
to slide under it,
then I took it
outside to a new
home on the hostas,

the lawyer's bill
for amending our wills
listing two of my
nieces to speak
for us when we are

unable—I'd rather
be bitten fatally
by a large spider
either in our house,
our bed, or maybe

in the garden rather
than ending up
in one of those
places with wheeled
chairs and walkers lined up

like fake chariots
O spider be the
instrument of my
death, dispatching me
to the afterlife

of grass clippings,
spent tulips, pruned
rose canes, oak leaf
debris by the ravine's
moist delicious lip

Birthday Dinner

Against the tapestry of a meal with friends,
I spoke against my mother. And others spoke.

Three mothers who preferred brothers, singing praise,
or saying, "Quiet, let your brother speak first."

On the table, a gift of white tulips in a bowl.
Since then, I feel mother's anger at my words—

she's been gone thirteen years, but she stays.
Helen, Judy, and me—friends, we don't lie.

I was in kindergarten when the twins were born—
from then on, the boys were always first.

When I spoke against my mother, it was two
days till my birthday—she used to say

I was born on a stormy night. We say a lot
of stupid things in a lifetime, some we don't regret.

Against the tapestry of a meal—white tablecloths,
bottles of wine—we three clinked glasses, eye to eye.

How to Swallow the Snake

Start by gauging its length and your esophagus.

Examine skin and fangs.
Refuse to spit it out.

Counter the gag reflex with lavender honey.

Many people have sisters. They don't all
marry the right men.

Count the good times on one hand.

And finger the memories like rosary beads.

Your family's beliefs were touching
and involved kneeling in front of statues.

O blessed virgin Mary.

How many sisters do you have,
someone asks

Tell them one passed away.
Tell them another one's ailing.

Light the liturgical candles.
Get down on your knees.

Luxembourg Gardens: An Assay

I read about the woman
responsible for the garden but I do not see her
on bended knee planting tulips.

Today, workmen are re-aligning beds
with stakes, twine, and their sharp eyes.

At another border, a young woman
kneels, pulling weeds. She can tell leaf from leaf.

My mother's advice in spring—
wait until you can be sure
of its identity before pulling out.

Nothing explains the roving guards
carrying uzis. They have nothing to do
with gardens.

Not only tulips, bluebells, sweet William.
Fountains, lavish outpourings.

And then we saw trees, flowing
in fantastic shapes, one tree pruned
sideways like a man reclining in water.

For days we travel on water, following
ancient patterns.

We sleep and dream on the boat,
I wake, dreaming of dancing.

We leave the boat to walk, letting
the mistral wind blow its dust onto
our shoes and hair.

I am altered by the wind and the light.
Each day, stone upon stone.

Orpheus sings, notes silver
like water.

After Reading about the Orca and Its Calf

Maybe it isn't saltwater
that heals—

my mother's theory—

but the mere going down
to the sea, removing your shoes,

a way of humbling yourself

before forces larger than,
deeper than, stronger than.

Once I body-surfed in Lake Superior.

When a wave smashed me,
I crawled out of the water.

Maybe it isn't that we're cruel—

if we believe that all the other
creatures hurt too, what a weight

of grief. I regret killing the spider

on the gray dashboard of my car.
It looked for a home—

The Seattle Times said the orca carried her
calf for a week, refusing to let the dead thing

go. Finally she let the sea take it.

Self-Portrait with a Million Dollars

Near a painted boulder with names of teams, high schools, sits the exit
  we take now to the graves.

Near the hill scotch-broomed gold, that roaming place, the some-
  time swamp, where I see myself with my small brothers,

three of us holding hands.

Near the heart of it all, the family whole, before anyone
  was sundered, though Ann

was about to leave us—I glimpse her outside, leaning over to kiss
  a boy in a red car.

It was so long ago, there weren't zip codes or cell phones,
  or the internet—

and the World's Fair was in Seattle, our grandmother flying in
  elegant—hat and white gloves—from Boston.

Muscle memory holds so much, landscape memory, too.

That overpass, exit, boulder, hill—with a convoy motoring
  west, how for months I'd begged Father

to take us to see it—a million dollars in silver dollars
  coming out of the east, a police escort

guiding it to the fair.

Near the railing, next to Father, I stood watching while a semi
blew past, dirt kicking up, pollen, road dust, freeway still
being built—

a motor parade gone in an eye blink—I hadn't understood
I'd never see a single, silver, gleaming coin.

Wood Eternal

When I stood, looking out on dormant trees devoid of green,
when I saw decomposing leaves turning to bits, the worn path left
     by hooves of white-tailed deer,
when I heard they would bulldoze weeds and bushes where migrating
     monarch butterflies rest, all to build a wall to keep people out,
when the sale of public land to oil barons, to drillers, was approved and signed,
then my heart grew sore, my breath weak, and I took myself soon to the river,
called the dog to me and we stepped out together, we heard the belted
     kingfisher rattle its warning and fly ahead of us along the bank,
we crossed a bridge where muskrats gambol in water like children
     and feed on freshwater clams,
and we stopped at the bald cypress, now shedding but strong and stout
     with a trunk made of wood eternal, growing there
     undisturbed by moving water,
      day after living day.

After Seeing a Fir Down at a Nearby Cemetery

Neither the dead whose graves
                    the tree spans and covers

nor the nearby dead in neat rows,
                    maybe even the relatives

do not care, or know. Come
                    Memorial Day their eyes will open

at a cracked headstone.
                    But now the fir's luxurious

green softens iron-hard ground,
                    the marble markers toppled,

and the trunk lies prone as one
                    of the dead, now joined.

Once I told my husband how much
                    Christmas wreaths on graves

cheered me—red bows on circles
                    of green. Lay one there

for me, I almost said—
                    I don't desire that vaulted

dark, permanent as a strut
                    of a bridge, a building's footstep—

Burn me and set my spirit free,
                    ash in the ravine, or mud

of Lamberton Creek or
                    the Grand River. Let flowing

water flow, and the body's spirit that adored
                    motion, rocking—let it move.

Acknowledgments

Thanks to the editors of the following journals where some of these poems first appeared, sometimes in slightly different versions or with different titles.

The Adirondack Review: "Those at the Edge of Water"

Alaska Quarterly Review: "Provenance"

Asheville Poetry Review: "Every Spider I Save Could Be the Instrument"

Barrow Street: "Big White Streak"

Blackbird: "Diptych with Window View & Hiroshige Print," "How to Swallow the Snake," "Kubota Garden"

Bridge Eight: "After the Suicides"

Cave Wall: "My Beautiful Family," "Self-Portrait with a Million Dollars"

Connotations Press: "After Seeing a Fir Down at a Nearby Cemetery"

Dark Matter: A Journal of Natural Metaphor: "I Am Going to Start Living Like a Zen Priest"

Dunes Review: "Near the Tea House at Meijer Japanese Garden"

The Fourth River: "Controlled Burn," "Coveting the River Birch," "For the Atlas Moth," "In Praise of the Dickcissel," "Mallards at Rest"

The Galway Review: "After the Darkest Year"

Inkwell: "Barred Owl"

Nelle: "After Reading about the Orca and Its Calf," "Love Song for Physics and the Nude," "Psychology of Travel"

New Letters: "Coaster," "Threnody"

North American Review: "After Failure," "Birthday Dinner"

Plume: "Canine Elegy," "Les Rochers de Belle-Ile"

Split Rock Review: "Sibelius While an Oak Topples"

upstreet: "At Random I Open the Book on Waking, Dreaming, Being to the Chapter on Dying"

Valparaiso Poetry Review: "Feasting, Then Falling," "When the Hawk Refuses to Fly"

"Doughnut Ghazal" was published in *The Book of Donuts,* eds. Jason Lee Brown and Shanie Latham (Terrapin Books, 2017)

"Thank a Gardener, a Perennial, a Bee" was reprinted in *Plume 6,* ed. Daniel Lawless, 2018.

"My Last Brother's Last Son" was reprinted in *Plume 8,* Daniel Lawless, 2020.

The poems published in *The Fourth Review* won the journal's folio competition in fall 2019 and were featured together in that issue.

About the Author

Patricia Clark is the author of *The Canopy* (Terrapin Books, 2017), her fifth book of poetry which won the 2018 PSV Book of the Year Award, and three chapbooks, including *Deadlifts* (New Michigan Press, 2018). She teaches in the Writing Department at Grand Valley State University in Michigan where she is also the university's poet in residence. She has won *The Fourth River's* Folio Competition, *Mississippi Review's* Poetry Prize, second prize in the Pablo Neruda/Hardiman Prize from *Nimrod*, and was the co-winner of Poetry Society of America's Lucille Medwick Prize. She has completed residencies at The MacDowell Colony, the Virginia Center for the Creative Arts, the Ragdale Colony, and The Tyrone Guthrie Center in Annaghmakerrig, Ireland. She was also the poet laureate of Grand Rapids, Michigan from 2005-2007, and for many years she coordinated Poetry Night, part of GVSU's Fall Arts Celebration.

www.patriciafclark.com

CPSIA information can be obtained
at www.ICGtesting.com
Printed in the USA
LVHW090845051020
667943LV00002B/142

9 781947 896277